ACCOUNTING
MANAGEMENT
— FOR —
SMALL BUSINESS
OWNERS

PIYUSH JAIN

INDIA • SINGAPORE • MALAYSIA

Notion Press

Old No. 38, New No. 6
McNichols Road, Chetpet
Chennai - 600 031

First Published by Notion Press 2020
Copyright © Piyush Jain 2020
All Rights Reserved.

ISBN 978-1-64805-676-5

Images Source: Google Images

Contents

About the Author

Piyush Jain is an author, coach, & full time consultant He has over 15 years of experience working in some of the largest companies of the world viz. Dun & Bradstreet, British Oil & Natural Gas Ltd., Stellar Furniture to name a few. Currently, he is based in Indore (M.P.), cleanest city of India running his firm D.J.Consultants helping the young entrepreneurs in the field of Accounts, Taxation & Investments.

Introduction

The main purpose of writing this book is to provide awareness and general guidance regarding how to start your own business and explains all the required knowledge, while deciding a business.

While it is a summary of the big picture as how you can have full guidance of various business procedure. For details I am always available on piyushcoach@gmail.com

What's there in it for Me

This course is designed for all those people who want to enter business or struggling after entering the business especially related to accounts & tax, I would be covering:

- ▲ Should I venture into business or not?

- ▲ What type of business entity is better for me i.e. Sole Proprietorship, Limited Liability Company, One Person Company or Private Limited Company?

- ▲ Types of Registrations Required viz. Gumasta, Municipal Corporation Certificate, Trademark License, PF, ESIC, GST Registration & PAN Card

- ▲ Software to use – Which is better Tally, Quick Books, Zoho Books or ERP?

- ▲ Basic Accounting Knowledge – What is Debit & Credit, Trial Balance, Cash Flow Statement, P&L A/c, Inventory, Balance Sheet?

- ▲ Simplifying Taxes – Income Tax & GST are they one and the something, if not, what is their importance in business?

- ▲ Company Formation – One Person Company vs. Private Limited Company, documents required & cost involved?

- ▲ Requirement of Audit – Types of Audit & Who can conduct it and its use?

- ▲ What is the difference between Chartered Accountant & Company Secretary, when to hire them?

Well, guys, there's a lot to cover, so let's move on to the next chapter to learn each of the above topics in detail...

Chapter 1

Should I Venture Into Business or Not?

Well, that's an independent choice, running a business have its own advantage over doing a job, there are both pros & cons, let's have a look:

Business	Doing Job
Independent-Own Boss	Working for Someone
Not a fixed Revenue	Fixed Income Every Month
Free to develop one's own creativeness & skills as required	Working as per the given job description
Will have to learn and be aware in all areas of business – HR, Finance, Admin, Sales Management	No such worry
Can increase revenue by increasing Turnover & profits	Income will grow by bonus & promotions only
Free to take holidays & go on vacations	Depend on company's leaves policy and boss mood

As told earlier, choosing business as a carrier has its advantage, now let us move to another chapter to learn how to proceed in business, if chosen business as a carrier.

Chapter 2

What Type of Business Entity is Better for Me?

This is important, why? Because your whole business future depends on it. First of all, we will have to understand different forms of business to move forward:

⮝ Sole Proprietorship:

The sole proprietorship is the simplest business form under which one can operate a business. It is not a legal entity. It simply refers to a person who owns the business and is personally responsible for its debts.

Some examples are small businesses such as single person art studio, a local grocery store, or an IT consultant service. The moment you start offering goods & services, you form a sole proprietorship firm.

⮝ Limited Liability Partnership (LLP):

When two or more persons join hands to run a business, it is called Partnership. LLP is the extended version of Partnership, here the partners will have to get their deed registered and each partner is not responsible or liable for another partner's misconduct or negligence.

⮝ One Person Company (OPC):

The One Person Company (commonly known as OPC) is the type of entity which is owned and managed by a single person. It is governed by the Indian Companies Act, 2013.

Some of the advantages are:

- Independent Existence
- Easy Funding & Loans

- Limited Liability
- Director & Shareholder can be same person
- Increase trust & prestige
- Easy online registration process

⅄ Private Limited Company (PLC):

A private limited company is a business entity held by small group of people. It is registered for a pre-defined objects and owned by a group of members called as Shareholders.

The business entity gets recognized as a PRIVATE LIMITED COMPANY after it is registered under Companies Act,2013. The governing body is Ministry of Corporate Affairs (MCA).

Benefits are as follows:

- Limited liability of shareholders
- Credibility & Reputation
- Management & Ownership are separate
- Perpetual Succession
- Ease in obtaining Funds & Loans

Well, care must be taken while choosing type of business entity

If we choose to run a sole proprietorship or also called as Firm (by some), it is very-very easy to form and manage but when getting funds or loans from banks, it is quite difficult because trust don't come easy as owner & business are one & same here and also most of the firm are not -audited.

We would be learning about audit in coming chapters.

Similarly, choosing a PLC or also called as Company has its pros and cons, getting funds is easy but we have to follow a lot of regularities like getting books of accounts audited, compulsory filing of Income Tax Returns, Hiring Company Secretary and maintaining Minutes of Meetings etc.

Now, let us move to the next chapter to understand the types of registrations required.

Chapter 3

Types of Registrations Required

Once we have chosen the type of entity whether Sole Proprietorship/LLP/PLC, we have to obtain certain licences/registrations, below we will look into some of the commonly applicable licences:

⋏ Trade Licenses:

It is a certificate/document which grants the permission to carry on trade or business in a particular area/location. The core objective of issuing this is to control the locations by restricting the people from executing certain type of businesses from their home locations to maintain the business environment & locality environment.

These are issued by licensing department of the municipal corporations. It grants permission by way of letter or certificate to carry on any business or trade where it is located. The issuance of certificate varies from state to state and common examples are Gumasta, Shop& Establishment License, FSSAI (related to food items) term may differ as per language of state.

⋏ Trademark, Patent & Copyright:

- Copyright protects your art and writings
- Trademark protects your name, symbols or slogans for product or services
- Patent protects your inventions & designs

⋏ Provident Fund & ESIC Registrations:

- PF is mandatory for all businesses with 20 or more persons. All employees become eligible for PF rights from the commencement of business and onus of deduction & payment of PF is with the employer.

- ESIC is must for entities employing 20 or more persons. It is required for employees earning less than Rs. 15,000/- pm. It is a self-financing social security & health insurance for Indian Workers.

⅄ PAN & TAN:

If forming Company, we have to obtain separate PAN and Tax Account Number (TAN) for deducting taxes and submitting to Government.

These are some of the licenses/registrations which business required to operate, they also require GST Registrations which we would be learning in coming chapters.

Chapter 4

Types of Accounting Software's

A person going to start a business or who has recently started his own business must be very conscious concerning accounting software, non-managing of financial records in the proper & systematic way is the primary cause of business failures in India.

Commonly managed software's are:

⋏ Tally:

It is the most commonly used accounting software across India. It is an offline tool and most preferred by Chartered Accountants. The only demerit is if it is installed in one computer, we cannot install in other and it's a bit expensive, also if we use demo/education version we will not be able to use all the features available in Tally.

We can create several business entities (for e.g. Company A, B, C, D etc) in One Tally software within the same computer.

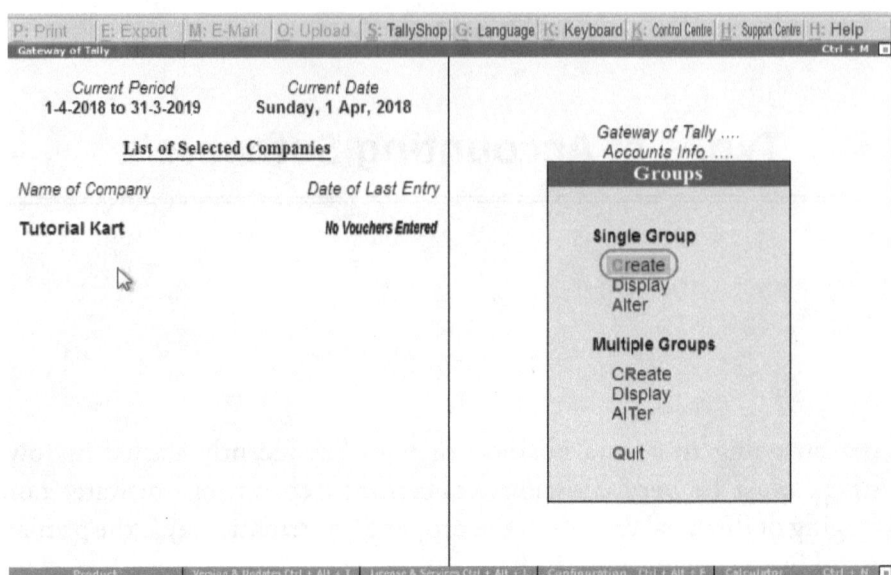

⤣ Quick Books:

It is the online accounting software, you can operate it from any system around the world, the only requirement is Internet, Login ID & Password. It comes at a yearly payment price (quite economical) and it is very good for service-oriented businesses. For each of the company (say if we are having company A, B, C & D) we would be requiring separate licence to use it (for each of the company A, B, C & D).

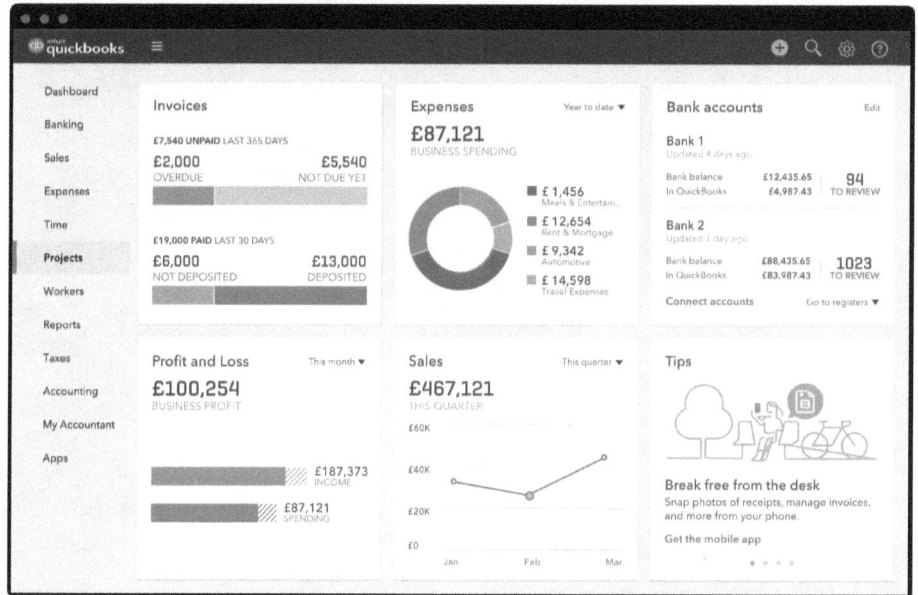

⊿ Zoho Books:

It is also an online accounting software that you can operate from anywhere (just like Quick Books). Advantage it has got that it is also a CRM software i.e. you can operate your entire Customer & Sales related work from this s software apart from Accounting & Tax work.

 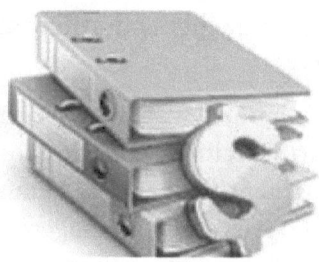

⋏ ERP:

Enterprise Resource Planning Software is designed to integrate the main functional areas of an organization's business processes into a unified system. It includes core software components, often called modules, for each department there is a separate module viz. HR module, Finance Module, Sales Module, Admin Module, Marketing Module, Production Module, Inventory Module. It is mainly used by big businesses having various branches and offices and it is quite expensive and requires expertise to operate.

In simple words, if we are a big company and having our branches in various cities then we would be requiring ERP softwares. Here, each department (Sales, HR, Finance/Accounts, Purchases) can enter their data in the system and management sitting in Head Office can download the consolidated report anytime as and when required. (Common Examples are Microsoft Dynamics, Tally.ERP etc)

These are commonly used accounting software. The only requirement is we should know English & little accounting knowledge.

Chapter 5

Basics of Accounts

It plays a vital role in running a business as it helps us in tracking income & expenditure through which we can know whether we are running our business in profit or incurring losses.

We should be familiar with some common terminology:

⋏ Debit & Credit:

Many times we hear this jargon and wonder what they are?

They are nothing but synonyms for left side & right side in Accounting i.e. whether expenses or incomes should be recorded on the left side or right side in Accounting Software.

Commonly used principle:

- Debit all Expenses & Assets – It means all expenses & assets should be recorded in left side
- Credit All Revenue & Liabilities – It means all income & liabilities should be recorded in right side

New Journal

Date	20 Oct 2017
Reference#	12
Notes	Transfer of funds
Journal Type	☐ Cash based journal ⓘ
Currency	AED- UAE Dirham ⌄

Account	Description	Contact (AED)		Debits	Credits	
Petty Cash ⌄	Description	Sayir Enterprises	× ⌄	1000		⊝
Office Supplies ⌄	Description	Global Electronics	× ⌄		1000	⊝

+ Add another line

	Sub Total	1000.00	1000.00
	Total (AED)	1000.00	1000.00

Attach File(s) 📎 Upload File ▾
You can upload a maximum of 5 files, 5MB each

Save   Cancel

⅄ Assets:

An item or property owned by businesses, which is having value and available to meet debts, commitments or legacies. For e.g. Furniture, Cash, Stock, Computers, Vehicles, Building, etc.

- Short-Term or Current Assets – Hold by business for less than 1 year period (E.g. Cash, Debtors, Stocks etc.)
- Long-Term or Fixed Assets – Owned by business for greater than 1 year (For e.g. Furniture, Office Premise, Vehicles etc.)

⅄ Liabilities:

These are the company's legal financial debts or obligations that arise during the course of business operations. It is settled over time through the transfer of economic benefits including money, goods & services. In simple words what business owes or has to pay to maintain continuity of its business. Common examples are Bank Loans, Creditors, etc. Just like Assets, liabilities too are Short & Long-Term in Nature.

⋏   Inventory:

In business goods or products are brought for sale, these are nothing but unsold goods or products lying in the godown. They are commonly called as STOCK.

⋏   Cash Flow Statement:

In business, cash is the king, businessman should always know his cash position to save his business from failure. Below is the simple cash flow statement.

YOUR COMPANY NAME		
CASH FLOW STATEMENT		
CASH FLOW STATEMENT AS ON 12/31/2015		
OPENING BALANCE OF CASH AT BEGINNING OF THE YEAR ₹ 15,700		
CASH FLOW OPERATIONS		
CASH RECEIVED FROM		
CLIENTS OR CUSTOMERS	₹ 925,000	
OTHER MISCELLANEOUS OPERATION	₹ 123,000	₹ 1,048,000
CASH PAID FOR		
PURCHASE OF INVENTORY	₹ 300,000	
GENERAL AND ADMINISTRATIVE EXPENSE	₹ 75,000	
SALARY/WAGES EXPENSES	₹ 150,000	
INTEREST PAID BORROWINGS	₹ 12,000	
INCOME TAX PAID	₹ 15,500	₹ 552,500
NET CASH FLOW OPERATIONS		₹ 495,500

⋏   Profit & Loss Account:

Every businessman works for earning profit. He/She can know whether his entity is earning profit or running in loss through Profit or Loss Account,

It is calculated deducting all its Expenses from its Revenue/Turnover, if revenue is greater than expenses we earn profit or else loss. It is usually prepared for entire month/quarter/year. Below is the simple Profit & Loss Account Statement.

Income statement for XYZ business for the period ending 31st of December 2010	Budgeted	Actual
INCOME	$	$
Services rendered	100,000	94,600
EXPENSES		
Salaries	25,000	25,000
Telephone & internet	6,500	6,500
Water & electricity	14,000	16,000
Property rates and taxes	1,000	1,000
Insurance	7,300	7,300
Advertising costs	1,000	1,000
Fuel	1,800	2,500
Stationery	500	412
Bank charges / interest paid	600	654
Tax expense	3,000	3,414
NET PROFIT	39,300	30,820

⋏ Balance Sheet:

A person should be aware about how much assets & liabilities are there in his business. It can be obtained from the Balance Sheet. It is prepared at a specific point in time, e.g. as on date. Say 31st March or 31st of every month (if prepared monthly). In Balance Sheet, Assets are always equal to Liabilities (golden Rule).

Below is the simple Balance Sheet Format:

Balance sheet for XYZ business on the 31st of December 2010		
	$	$
ASSETS		
Non-current assets		2,150,000
Land and buildings	2,000,000	
Furniture	12,000	
Machinery	18,000	
Investments	120,000	
Current assets		10,000
Inventory	1,000	
Debtors / receivables	3,200	
Bank and cash	5,800	
TOTAL ASSETS		2,160,000
EQUITY AND LIABILITIES		
Owner's equity		1,700,000
Capital	1,700,000	
Non-current liabilities		440,000
10% Loan	440,000	
Current liabilities		20,000
Creditors / payables	20,000	
TOTAL EQUITY AND LIABILITIES		2,160,000

So, we have learned in detail about various terminology of Accounts, now we move to our next chapter to learn about TAXES.

If you have any doubts or questions, please email me on piyushcoach@ gmail.com.

Chapter 6

Simplifying Taxes

A businessperson should always know about the taxes. Taxes are nothing but a source of revenue to Government which it spends on public welfare like building roads, dams, satellite, etc.

In India, there are two types of taxes levied, first Direct Tax which is Income Tax and other is Indirect tax which is Goods & Service Tax or GST, we will learn about them one by one.

Income Tax

It is the tax which is levied on our income. For Salaried persons, it is deducted from their salary and for businesspersons, it is levied on their profits. Some things which we should be familiar with are:

- Financial Year – It is the year in which person earns his revenue, In India, it is from 1st April to 31st March, e.g. say 1st April'2019 to 31st March'2020 will be called FY 2019–2020.

- Assessment Year – It comes after Financial Year. This is the time in which the income earned is assessed and taxed. For FY 2019–2020, AY would be 2020–2021.

- Form 16 – It is a statement which states the income earned and tax deducted by employed personnel. This is provided by the company to an employee and with the help of form 16 an employee can file his/her Income Tax Returns commonly called ITR.

- TDS – Every month employer while paying salary to his employee, deducts tax, this is called as Tax Deduction on Source

(TDS), employer must file TDS Return, it has details of each employees PAN, Salary & Tax Deducted. In the end when the employee files his/her ITR, then only he can come to know whether he must pay tax or claim a refund from the Income Tax Department.

- 26AS Form – This form is available from Income Tax Website https://www.incometaxindiaefiling.gov.in/home. It states the income on which TDS has been deducted.

- Tax Slab – Tax is levied as below:

Latest Income Tax Slab Rates for FY 2020-21 AY 2021-22 (www.basunivesh.com)			
If you are claiming deductions and exemptions			
Income Slab	Individuals (Aged below 60 Yrs)	Senior Citizens (Aged 60 Yrs and above but below 80 Yrs)	Super Senior Citizens (Aged 80 Yrs and above)
Up to Rs.2,50,000	Nil	Nil	Nil
Rs.2,50,001 to Rs.3,00,000	5%	Nil	Nil
Rs.3,00,001 to Rs.5,00,000	5%	5%	Nil
Rs.5,00,001 to Rs.10,00,000	20%	20%	20%
Rs.10,00,001 and above	30%	30%	30%
If you are NOT claiming deductions and exemptions			
Income Slab	Income Tax Rate		
Up to Rs.2,50,000	Nil		
Rs.2,50,001 to Rs.5,00,000	5% (with Tax Rebate Under Sec.87A)		
Rs.5,00,001 to Rs.7,50,000	10%		
Rs.7,50,001 to Rs.10,00,000	15%		
Rs.10,00,0001 to Rs.12,50,000	20%		
Rs.12,50,001 to Rs.15,00,000	25%		
Rs.15,00,000 and above	30%		

Tax slab for Partnership Firm is at 30% + Surcharge of 12% of Tax where total income exceeds Rs. 1 Crore

And, for Companies it is 25% + Surcharge 7% where income is between 1 Cr.-10 Cr. and 12% above Rs. 10Cr. + Health & Education Cost at 4% of income tax.

I have helped several start-ups and individuals in TAX PANNING & ITR FILING, I can be reached at piyushcoach@gmail.com if you require Tax Planning or want to file your ITR.

Now we will learn about various Income Tax Return (ITR) Forms:

Income Tax Return is a form in which an individual file his total income, his eligible investments (for deductions) and calculate his tax to pay or refund to get and submit it to the Income Tax Department.

Various Forms used for Tax filing are:

⊿ ITR 1 (Sahaj) – Resident Individual having income less Rs. 50 lakhs from:

- Salary/Pension
- Other Sources viz. Bank Interest
- One House Property Viz. Rental

⊿ ITR 2 – Income from:

- Every income from ITR 1 > Rs. 50 lakhs
- Capital gain from sale of House Property or Shares
- More than one house property
- Foreign Income/Foreign Asset
- Holding Directorship in a Company
- Holding unlisted equity shares

⊿ ITR 3 – Income from:

- Every income from ITR 2
- Business/Profession
- As a partner in a firm
- Presumptive income till Rs. 50 lakhs (here income is calculated on estimation basis)

⊿ ITR 4 – Every income under ITR 1 and Presumptive Income under (Total Income > Rs. 50 lakhs)

- Salary/Pension
- Other Sources
- One House Property

⋏ ITR 5 – Applicable to:

- Firms
- LLPs
- AOP's
- BOI's

⋏ ITR 6 – Applicable to:

- Companies not claiming exemption u/s 11

⋏ ITR 7 – Applicable to person/companies:

- U/s 139 (4A)
- U/s 139 (4B)
- U/s 139 (4C)
- U/s 139 (4D)

Things to take care while filing ITR

- The filing date of salaried persons is 31st July after which income tax department levies fine.
- The filing date of ITR by business falling under the category of Tax Audit is 30th September.
- Always use correct ITR forms for filing your income or else ITR will become invalid
- There is always the option of rectifying the ITR if any mistake or omission has been done
- It should be noted that ITD allows to file ITR for current FY only and now no one can file ITR for any of the previous FYs.
- Refund of TDS or taxes paid can be claimed only through ITR.
- Aadhar & PAN must be linked for filing ITR
- Aadhar & PAN must be updated in your bank account for claiming refunds

- Now-a-days e-filing of ITR can be done but for that, your Aadhar must have valid working mobile number.

This was all related to Direct Tax and now we will understand Indirect Tax.

Goods & Service Tax

Commonly known as GST, it is an indirect tax and came into effect on 1ˢᵗ July,2017 after replacing VAT/CST/Excise/Service Tax. It is levied on supply of goods & services in India.

▲ Benefits – Introduction of GST has helped reduce tax rates, remove multiple point of taxation, and increase revenues. Basically, a uniform tax system has made India a common market and boosted trade, commerce & export.

▲ Types – GST is divided into 4 types

- CGST – Central Goods & Service Tax
- SGST – State Goods & Service Tax
- IGST – Integrated Goods & Service Tax
- UTGST – Union Territory Goods & Service Tax

▲ When GST is Compulsory? – When the turnover of the business exceeds Rs. 40 lakhs (Rs. 20lakhs for North Eastern and Hill States), it is mandatory to register under GST. For certain business viz. doing inter-state business, it is mandatory to register, and turnover criteria becomes invalid. After registration, entity gets GST Certificate and Number which it has to display on its Name Board and Invoices always (else fine/penalty can be imposed)

▲ Types of GST Returns – Various types are as follows:

- GSTR 1 – Return for Outward Supplies
- GSTR 2 – Return for Inwards Supplies
- GSTR 2A – Read Only Document
- GSTR 3B – Summary of Inward & Outward Supplies

- GSTR 4 – Return for Composition Dealers
- GSTR 5 – Non-Resident taxable Persons
- GSTR 6 – Return for Input Service Distributors
- GSTR 7 – Taxpayer deducting TDS
- GSTR 8 – E-Commerce Operator collecting TCS
- GSTR 9 – Annual Return for normal taxpayer
- GSTR 9A – Annual Return for Composition Dealers
- GSTR 10 – Registered Person whose GST Registration gets cancelled

⅄ Late Fees in GST:

Particulars	Late Fees (Rs.)
Normal Return (GSTR 1, 3B, 4, 5, 5A & 6)	Rs. 50/- per day till date of filing
Nil Return (GSTR 1, 3B, 4, 5, 5A)	Rs. 20/- per day till date of filing

So, this was related to GST for any queries, always feel free to contact me. One thing to note for GST is that Audit can only be done by Chartered Accountant whereas Returns can be filed by self, return preparers or CA's.

In next chapter, we will learn about how to form a Company…

Chapter 7

How to form or Incorporate Company in India?

As discussed earlier, we can form One Person Company or Private Limited Companies, Steps to form companies are discussed as follows:

- Obtain Director Identification Number (DIN)for proposed Directors of the new Company

- Obtain Digital Signature Certificate (DSC)for proposed Directors of the new Company

- Filing the proposed name of Company for approval to the Registrar of the Companies (ROC)

- Get the Memorandum of Association (MOA) & Article of Association(AOA) printed

- Pay requisite stamp duties online

- File all incorporation forms and documents online including MOA & AOA

- Obtain the Certificate of Incorporation (COI)

- Request and obtain Certificate to Commence Operation, if required

It can take from 7–40 working days for company formation. The actual time and procedure may vary with city and state and the nature of the business.

In theory, forming a PLC is easy but procedures and form are complicated, so always take the help of Company Secretory for Incorporating Company in India.

We have helped various start-ups in forming PLC & OPC, so if you guys need any help, please reach me on piyushcoach@gmail.com

Things to take care while forming of PLC in India:

- Registered Business Name

- Registered Business Office

- Shareholders: Minimum 2 and maximum of 200 for PLC

- Share Capital: The company must be formed with a stated, nominal share capital divided into shares of fixed amounts. The minimum authorized capital is Rs. 100,000/-

- Memorandum of Association (MOA): It is the company's charter. It states Co's name, the situation of its registered office, its share capital, the fact that liability is limited and most important the object for which the company is formed. It must be signed by at least 3 shareholders.

- Article of Association (AOA): It contains the internal regulations of the company, the relation of the company to its shareholders, and the relationship between the shareholders.

- Certificate of Incorporation: This is the document, which the ROC issues to you once it has approved your choice of name and memorandum. When you receive this document your company legally exists and is ready to trade.

- Auditors: Every PLC must appoint CA to get his books of accounts audited.

- Accounts & Registers: Every PLC must maintain books of accounts and Registers viz. A register of members and share ledger; a register of directors and secretaries; a register of share transfers; a register of charges; a register of debenture holders; a book can be purchased to hold all of the above.

- Company Seal: All companies must have an engraved seal. This must be impressed on share certificates and must be used whenever the company has to execute a deed.

Minimum cost to form a company in India is Rs.15,000/- but than it would vary from state, nature and type of business.

Wow, that was huge!! now in next chapter we would be covering about AUDIT, why & how?

Chapter 8

Audit in Business

An audit is an evaluation or examination of something by a person or a group of persons. In terms of Accounts, it is examination or inspection of books of accounts by a third party followed by physical checking of inventory to make sure all departments are following documented system of recording transactions.

Here we would be talking mainly about Internal & External Audit

- Internal Audit: It is conducted at the request of internal management in order to check the health of the company's finances and analyze the operational efficiency of the organization. It may be performed by an independent party or company's own staff. Some of the e.g. are Management Audit, Stock Audit etc.

- External Audit: It is also termed as statutory audit and it is conducted for each financial year. The two most common types are:

    - Tax Audit – It is required U/s 44AB of ITA, 1961. It is conducted by qualified CA and following points should be taken care:

        - Every business whose turnover exceeds Rs. 10 million in any previous FY;

        - Professions whose turnover exceeds Rs. 5 million in any previous FY have to mandatory conduct Tax Audit

- The provisions are applicable to everyone be it sole proprietorship firm, partnership firm, a company or any other entity.

- Non-compliance attracts penalty of Rs.10,000 or 0.5% of turnover whichever is lower.

- It is to be obtained by 30th September after the end of previous FY.

- Company Audit: It is mandatory for all types of companies whether PLC or OPC as per Companies Act, 2013 irrespective of the nature of the business or turnover. Things to take care:

  - It can be done only a qualified CA;

  - Auditor checks the books of accounts, ledgers, cash flow accounts, p&L a/c and balance sheet and provides his opinion that "It provides True & Fair view or not".

  - After completion, it provides seal & signed report.

  - Audit Report plays a vital role when obtaining external finances for the company.

Well, this chapter was about audit, in next chapter we will learn about role of Chartered Accountant & Company Secretary.

Chapter 9

Chartered Accountant & Company Secretary

Criteria	Chartered Accountants	Company Secretary
Skills Required	Accounting, IT, Analytical Ability and Business Acumen	Proficiency in law and management, communication, accounting & auditing
Statutory Body in India	The Institute of Chartered Accountants of India (ICAI)	The Institute of Company Secretary of India (ICSI)
Scope	The field of finance, corporate finance, management consultancy, tax compliance and change management.	Can work in Government Accounts or law department or become MD or CMD and be part of BOD
Mandatory	Compulsory for all Companies to perform Financial Audit	Compulsory for Business after certain turnover to appoint CS to perform secretarial work.

Remarks

Well, guys this was all related to business, hope you would have enjoyed all the sessions, in the end I would just like to say that If you have any queries, I am always available on **piyushcoach@gmail.com**.

Understanding entire accounts takes time & effort, students study it under CA, CS & MBA. I have tried to cover maximum possible contents so that a person starting his new business becomes aware and do not suffer because of his lack of knowledge. While effort has been taken to cover as much details as possible in summarized way but limitations are possible.

It is my first book and this topic is very near to my heart, so request you to please provide your comments as a review to my book.

Thank You all for purchasing & reading this book.

HAVE A NICE BUSINESS AHEAD!!!